IMAGES
of America

THE COAST GUARD
IN MASSACHUSETTS

The Coast Guard, under that name, has been on duty in Massachusetts since 1915. (Paul Rooney.)

ON THE COVER: Hurricane Carol stood New Bedford on its end, but the Coast Guard was there to help save lives, alleviate pain, and rebuild. (United States Coast Guard.)

IMAGES
of America

THE COAST GUARD
IN MASSACHUSETTS

Donald J. Cann and John J. Galluzzo
Foreword by Capt. W. Russell Webster,
USCG (Ret.)

ARCADIA
PUBLISHING

Amazon

1. 917.44

17.50

12/4

Published by Arcadia Publishing
Charleston, South Carolina

Printed in the United States of America

Library of Congress Control Number: 2010943216

For all general information, please contact Arcadia Publishing:
Telephone 843-853-2070
Fax 843-853-0044
E-mail sales@arcadiapublishing.com
For customer service and orders:
Toll-Free 1-888-313-2665

Visit us on the Internet at www.arcadiapublishing.com

*This book is dedicated to all Guardians who serve or have
served along the Massachusetts shore. Bravo Zulu!*

CONTENTS

FOREWORD

Precarious seas off the Massachusetts coast have long created an environment ripe for tragedy, unheralded heroism, and innovation, linking the commonwealth to important eras of the past, as well as the contemporary culture of the Coast Guard.

In 2007, the Coast Guard recognized its milestone one millionth life saved since its inception in 1790 and published its "top 10" all-time rescues. Listed third among all actions was what some have characterized as the greatest small-boat rescue—the saving of 32 seamen in 1952 from the broken 502-foot tanker *Pendleton* off Chatham on Cape Cod.

All four Coast Guardsmen involved received the coveted Gold Lifesaving Medal, and the boat's coxswain, Bernard Webber, is now the namesake for the service's first 153-foot coastal Sentinel-class cutter. On average, five or six Gold Lifesaving Medals are given out each year to members of the public to recognize extraordinary acts of heroism. Historical records indicate Massachusetts' rescuers comprise a good number of the award recipients. Gen. George S. Patton received medal recognitions for assisting three distressed boys off Salem in the 1930s.

Among the commonwealth maritime heroes is the notable Joshua James, credited with saving nearly 1,000 mariners. Another notable was the quirky heroine and the service's most peculiar and long-tenured volunteer rescuer, Mildred "Madaket Millie" Carpenter Jewett. Jewett, despite having poor eyesight, raised and trained military working dogs during World War II. Millie has been credited with towing a live mine ashore and with killing a blue shark with a pitchfork after Hurricane Carol misdirected the unfortunate creature into Nantucket waters.

But, beyond an environment that bred maritime heroes, the Coast Guard in Massachusetts has been home to some of the service's first coastal rescue huts and lifeboat stations. It also had an early air station and the last lightship in service, the nation's first lighthouse (and the only remaining lighthouse to be congressionally mandated to provide a modern-day light keeper), and some of Alexander Hamilton's earliest revenue cutters.

A good portion of what we know today in terms of rescue equipment and techniques, including cardio pulmonary resuscitation, was gained through the wellspring of intellectual energy from the Humane Society of the Commonwealth of Massachusetts, a forerunner organization of the modern Coast Guard, which continues to fund cutting-edge survival and lifesaving training and equipment to this very day.

Donald J. Cann and John J. Galluzzo artfully bring the commonwealth's role and importance in Coast Guard history to life with their handsome images. Encompassing lightships, lighthouses, tenders, small boats, cutters, and air stations, this book celebrates the Coast Guard's service in a state with a storied and proud maritime heritage.

—Capt. W. Russell Webster, USCG (Ret.)

Capt. W. Russell Webster, USCG (Ret.) retired in 2003 after 26 years of military service. He was the 1998–2001 Woods Hole rescue commander. He oversaw the Coast Guard's operational response to the 1999 air crashes of John F. Kennedy Jr.'s small airplane off Martha's Vineyard and Egypt Air flight 990 off Nantucket. From 2001 until his retirement, he was the chief of operations for the Northeast Coast Guard District and oversaw the regional response to the September 11th terrorist attacks. In 2010, he was recognized by former commandant Thad Allen and the Foundation for Coast Guard History for his 30-year commitment to service history and heritage.

ACKNOWLEDGMENTS

The authors have numerous people and organizations to thank for helping to make this book come together, from photograph sources to those folks who tipped us off to angles of the story of the Coast Guard in Massachusetts we had not yet considered. In no particular order, they are as follows: Boston Harborfest, Inc.; BMCS Jason Holm, USCG; BMCS David Considine, USCG; LCDR Paul J. Rooney Jr., USCG; the Newburyport Harbor Commission; Marcia D. Melnyk of the Custom House Maritime Museum in Newburyport; Richard Ryder of Eastham; Richard Boonisar of South Dennis; Glenn Stockwell of Orleans; Bill Quinn of Orleans; David Ball and Fred Freitas of the Scituate Historical Society; the Old Colony Club of Plymouth; Jeremy Slavitz of Nantucket; the amazing team at the Trayser Museum of Coast Guard Heritage in Barnstable Village—Mickey Broadhurst, Bill Collette, and Jack McGrath; Laurel Guadazno of the Pilgrim Monument and Provincetown Museum; Joanie Gearin and the staff at the National Archives and Records Administration in Waltham, Massachusetts; BM1 Mike Faivre, USCG; the Coast Guard historian Robert M. Browning Jr. and his staff—Scott Price, Bill Thiesen, Chris Havern, Jeff Bowdoin and Nora Chidlow; Timothy Harrison, editor of *Lighthouse Digest*; David Gamage of Jay, Maine; BMC Paul G. Wells, USCG; PO Erich Silvoy, USCG; Sally Snowman, keeper of Boston Lighthouse; Capt. W. Russell Webster, USCG (Ret.); LCDR Barrett Thomas Beard, USCG (Ret.); Capt. John "Bear" Moseley, USCG (Ret.); CDR Maurice Gibbs, USN (Ret.) of Nantucket; Mark Wilkins, executive director of the Chatham Historical Society; and Mary Ann Gray, archivist for the Chatham Historical Society. For moral support and everything else an author needs, we thank Janet Cann and Michelle Galluzzo. Any errors or omissions are ours, not theirs.

INTRODUCTION

When it formed in 1915, the Coast Guard in Massachusetts had a lot to live up to. The commonwealth had a long history with its predecessor agencies, those organizations that came together to make the new entity, and there was an enormous amount of pride at stake.

The Coast Guard's early history is written mainly in the annals of three main organizations: the Revenue Cutter Service, the Life-Saving Service, and the Lighthouse Service. The former and the latter changed names several times over the course of their history, and the Revenue Cutter Service, in what would become Coast Guard tradition, transformed as the country needed it to. The Life-Saving Service lived up to its name, saving the lives of 186,000 mariners in distress at sea between 1871 and 1915.

That organization was patterned directly on a system of lifeboat and mortar stations that developed on the Massachusetts coastline between 1786 and the late 1840s. The Humane Society of the Commonwealth of Massachusetts, a gathering of doctors, merchants, philanthropists, and other Boston-area citizens concerned with the notion of reviving "the apparently drowned," met to pool resources and expertise. Their common labor eventually provided for a series of "humane houses" along the shore, huts of refuge designed to help shipwreck victims survive until help could arrive. The next step, proactive lifesaving offshore, symbolically came to life in 1807 with the placement of a lifeboat in Cohasset, though that boat was never used. A massive building effort in the 1840s, spurred by the tragic "Triple Hurricanes of 1839" that decimated Cape Cod's fishing fleets, culminated with the construction and manning of 18 volunteer lifeboat stations, located from the North Shore to Martha's Vineyard.

In 1848, the federal government, in an attempt to similarly defend the approaches to New York Harbor, appropriated $5,000 for "surfboats, rockets, and carronades" to be placed on the New Jersey and Long Island shores in the same pattern being used in Massachusetts. Through fits and starts, that organization eventually became the United States Life-Saving Service. The first federal stations in Massachusetts appeared on Cape Cod in 1872. Several commonwealth communities waited as many as 30 years for their local federally funded stations to be built. Local volunteer crews were still active, even into the 1920s, and oftentimes obviated the need for a second local lifesaving crew. In the end, however, the Humane Society phased out its lifeboat operations, and the Coast Guard took over that role permanently. In 1915, 31 Life-Saving Service stations instantly became US Coast Guard stations.

In January 1915, Pres. Woodrow Wilson created the Coast Guard by merging the Life-Saving Service and the Revenue Cutter Service. The Revenue Cutter Service formed in 1790, as the United States, that brand new entity, found that it needed to recoup millions of dollars in debt accrued during the Revolution. From the very outset, taxation would become a necessity. Smuggling, once patriotic, became prohibited and was suddenly unpatriotic. The new country needed the revenue from levies collected from goods moving in and out of US ports, and it needed an enforcement agency to be sure those taxes were paid. Enter the Revenue Cutter Service.

In 1791, responding to the call for 10 revenue cutters to be built, Newburyport shipbuilders launched the *Massachusetts*, a two-masted schooner to be under the leadership of John Foster Williams. Although not the first built, *Massachusetts* was the first to serve actively. She was also taken out of service after only 15 months, making her the shortest-serving of the first 10 cutters. But her mark on history had been made. Revenue cutters continued to serve the Massachusetts waters until 1915; their descendants, Coast Guard cutters, do so today.

Under Pres. William Howard Taft's watchword "unifunctionalism," the plan to bring the Life-Saving Service and the Revenue Cutter Service together (they actually operated together from 1871 to 1878, the former under the latter), came to fruition under President Wilson. At that time, the name Coast Guard was born.

More than two decades later, the Coast Guard took in its third main component (the Steamboat Inspection Service joined in 1922 and the Bureau of Marine Inspection in 1942), the Lighthouse Service. While the movement to maintain, oversee, and control the nation's lighted aids to navigation did not become a federal concern until 1789—under the same concern for tax revenue that created the Revenue Cutter Service—colonial lights had illuminated the waterways for more than half a century. Boston Lighthouse, the first lighthouse in what would become the United States, was built on Hull's Little Brewster Island in 1716.

And so our tale begins. The Coast Guard story in Massachusetts is one that concerns World War I, Prohibition, and World War II. It goes far offshore, with cutters from 65 feet to 270 feet. It runs the gamut of motor lifeboats from 26 feet to 36 feet to 44 feet to 47 feet. And it picks up the stories of Massachusetts' lighthouses and lightships in 1939, when those assets fell under the control of the Coast Guard.

It tells the story of the dramatic rescues of the *Pendleton* and *Fort Mercer* in 1952, the *Etrusco* in 1956, and the *Argo Merchant* 20 years after that. It survives the Hurricane of 1938 and Hurricane Carol in 1954. It's a tale of heroes and victims, of shipwrecks and storms and war, of those times of peace when the ocean decided to wage war.

The Coast Guard story in Massachusetts is so long and broad that it could not be included in its entirety in the pages of this book. Instead, this history covers 95 years of Coast Guard bravery in survey fashion, introducing the reader to the stations, the cutters, and the rescues that made the service so famous in state waters.

In the end, this book is just a beginning. Considering the 1,500 or so miles of Massachusetts coastline, it is a relationship that probably will never come to an end.

One

THE NORTH SHORE

The citizens of Newburyport have always had reason to celebrate their Coast Guard heritage. Depending on personal criteria, Newburyport may be called the birthplace of the service. The first revenue cutter, launched in 1791, was the *Massachusetts*, and it was Newburyport-built. Here, in 1973, during the opening festivities for the modern Merrimac River station, the Coast Guard band traveled to the town to walk in the community's parade. The act was symbolic of the North Shore's deep connection to the history of the service. (United States Coast Guard.)

At the time of the Life-Saving Service and Revenue Cutter Service merger in 1915, Plum Island hosted two shore stations. The northernmost station, at the mouth of the Merrimack River, was built in 1873 under the name Plum Island Life-Saving Station. In 1902, its name changed to Newburyport. (United States Coast Guard.)

The Newburyport station remained in service well into the middle of the 20th century, through numerous reconstructions and even erosion-forced moves. Maine Coast Guard historian David Gamage remembered the days when his father, pictured here at the helm of a 40-foot utility boat, ran the station. "Can you imagine," Gamage asked, "what is was like in high surf crossing that bar in this craft?" (David Gamage.)

The Plum Island Life-Saving Station, originally known as Knobbs Beach, stood guard over the southern end of the 11-mile-long stretch of sand. The opposite ends of the island, as today, were a study in contrasts. The southern station was in an unpopulated wildlife refuge. The northern station sat surrounded by summer cottages. (United States Coast Guard.)

The station house in this photograph was built in the Race Point style, named for the first of its kind, which was built at Provincetown. The watchtower at right took on added significance during World War II, as Coast Guardsmen watched not only for ships in distress, but also enemy submarines. The drill pole in the foreground on the left served as a false ship's mast for beach apparatus (or breeches buoy) drills. (United States Coast Guard.)

In the midst of an urban renewal wave that struck Newburyport in the early 1970s, work began on a new station building that would consolidate the Coast Guard's efforts in the region. The building was dedicated, appropriately, on August 4, 1973. August 4 is recognized as the birthday of the Coast Guard. (Paul Rooney.)

The new site on Water Street, on the Merrimack River, which gives the current station its name, offered protection for the lifeboat crews from the crashing waves found on the outer beach. Faster, motor-driven boats such as the 44-foot motor lifeboat, 41-foot utility boat, and small Boston Whalers in this image assured rapid response to marine disasters. (United States Coast Guard.)

As with all Coast Guard units across the country, the Merrimack River crews have been ready to respond to danger at a moment's notice and to act "in the highest traditions of the United States Coast Guard." According to his official citation, on October 13, 1982, Kevin J. Galvin, boatswain's mate second class, "while serving as coxswain of Coast Guard Motor Life Boat (MLB) 44315, engaged in a rescue operation at the entrance to the Merrimac River, Newburyport, Massachusetts. Upon notification that a small boat had capsized 1/4 mile north of the north jetty with two people in the water, the MLB was dispatched. Demonstrating exceptional seamanship, Petty Officer Galvin guided the MLB across the river bar and headed into the 15-foot breaking seas. Arriving on scene, Petty Officer Galvin maneuvered his vessel as close as possible to people in the water, but due to the breaking seas and close proximity to the jetty, he made the decision to use a swimmer. With Petty Officer Galvin's expert boat handling, he held the vessel into the breaking seas while his crewmen rescued the 2 survivors." (Paul Rooney.)

Galvin's crewman, SN John A. Kallelis, performed outstanding deeds that same day. "Upon arriving on scene, Seaman Kallelis entered the 15-foot breaking seas and proceeded to swim to the two people. Reaching the closer one, approximately 30 feet from the MLB, Seaman Kallelis grabbed hold of him and they were hauled back aboard the MLB. Seaman Kallelis immediately swam back to, and rescued, the semiconscious second person. Seaman Kallelis demonstrated remarkable initiative, exceptional fortitude, and daring in spite of imminent danger in this rescue. Seaman Kallelis's unselfish actions, courage, and unwavering devotion to duty are most heartily commended and are in keeping with the highest traditions of the United States Coast Guard." Both men received the Coast Guard Medal for their heroism. (Trayser Museum.)

Rockport's Straitsmouth Life-Saving Station remained in service long past World War II. Built in the prominent Duluth-type architectural style (a replica station served at Salisbury Beach to the north), the station went through two name changes, from Davis Neck to Gap Cove to Straitsmouth. (United States Coast Guard.)

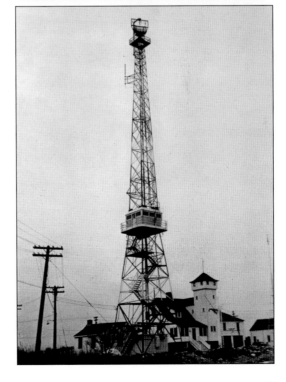

The station, on Marmion Way, remained in service until July 1964, and it later became a private home. The massive radio tower in the foreground doubled as an observation tower. (United States Coast Guard.)

Rockport's famous twin lights on Thacher's Island claim American Revolution roots, Civil War–era heroism, and National Historic Landmark status. By the time the Coast Guard took possession of the country's lighthouses in 1939, one tower, the north light, had been extinguished for seven years. The south tower remained active and manned until automation in 1979. Coast Guard keepers on the island spent much of their time alone or with dog mascots, but in 1967, they received an unexpected visitor. Joseph "the Animal" Barboza, being protected by the FBI as an informant in relation to organized crime activity in Massachusetts, was briefly quartered on the island. (United States Coast Guard.)

Gloucester's Eastern Point Lighthouse steadily glows on after more than a century and a half. The last keeper stationed there arrived in 1983, and in 1985, the light was automated. The Coast Guard retains the duplex as housing for service families. As shown here, lenses needed frequent inspection and cleaning at all lighthouses. (United States Coast Guard.)

Ten Pound Island off Gloucester features prominently in Coast Guard history, but not only for its lighthouse. The service operated a single small plane from the island, beginning in 1925, after moving from a brief stay at Squantum in Quincy. Aerial searches during this time had a single target—rumrunners. The lighthouse ceased operation as a manned station in 1956. Its lens can now be seen in the Maine Lighthouse Museum in Rockland, Maine. (United States Coast Guard.)

Gloucester's lights were not the only Coast Guard show in town. The old station, at Old House Cove, had a separate itinerant boathouse on Fresh Water Cove. The station building had its own launchway; the crew is pictured sliding down it. (United States Coast Guard.)

The old boathouse was designed in an age of "wooden boats and iron men," when surfmen and keepers rowed to rescues in oar-propelled lifeboats and surfboats. Here, in 1936, with classic fanciful Gloucester architecture in the background, the new boathouse foundation is prepared as the old boathouse awaits demolition. (United States Coast Guard.)

This aerial view encapsulates the entirety of the Gloucester Coast Guard Station. The road running behind the station continues to Dolliver's Neck. A 44-foot motor lifeboat rests alongside the launchway of the boathouse in the distance. (United States Coast Guard.)

The new Gloucester station, opened in the early 1970s in the shadow of Captain Solomon Jacobs Park, includes adequate dock space for the service to tie up cutters such as the 95-foot *Cape Cross*. The *Cape Cross* was home ported to Gloucester from 1969 to 1981. In 1977, during their tenure in Gloucester, the crew of the *Cape Cross* rescued the crew of the disabled fishing vessel *Chester Poling*. (United States Coast Guard.)

Squeezed off Gloucester's Ten Pound Island by their ever-increasing workload, the Coast Guard built Air Station Salem on Winter Island in 1935. Six years of operations honed the skills of the flyers based there, so that when the United States entered World War II on December 7, 1941, Salem provided an instant service to the country. In October 1944, the station became designated the first Air Sea Rescue station on the Eastern Seaboard. (Unite d States Coast Guard.)

At its height, Air Station Salem rotated 37 planes through its mission cycle, patrolling for enemy submarines, conducting medical evacuations, and responding to other marine emergencies. Among the many types of fixed-wing aircraft used for these missions was the Vought OS2U Kingfisher. The Kingfisher could fly for up to six hours and carry a depth charge, but no Coast Guard crew flying one was ever credited with a U-boat kill. (United States Coast Guard.)

The ramping up of Air Station Salem coincided with the rise of the helicopter. Early debaters argued whether or not coastal patrols were better suited to seaplanes or lighter-than-air craft (blimps); the point was eventually made moot by the helicopter. Here, at an open house at the air station in 1955, the capabilities of a Sikorsky HO4S are demonstrated. (United States Coast Guard.)

Air Station Salem served the mariners of the eastern seaboard until 1970, when it shut down in anticipation of the opening of Air Station Cape Cod at Otis Air Force Base. The move consolidated the operations of both the Salem and the Quonset Point, Rhode Island, detachment that had served under the Salem command. The men of the Salem Air Station left an amazing legacy. (United States Coast Guard.)

The Salem area sported several lighthouses to guide mariners through the various islands and into one of the United States' most important early harbors. Here, at Baker's Island Lighthouse in 1950, federal census takers Francis McCarthy and Thaddeus Mroz take their tally, which included Clifton L. Willis (boatswain's mate first class and lighthouse keeper), his wife, two kids, and two dogs. (United States Coast Guard.)

The lighthouse at Derby Wharf in Salem was automated in 1917, well before the Coast Guard's acceptance of the nation's lighthouses into their sphere of responsibility in 1939. From that point until 1977, the Coast Guard's role consisted of maintenance. In 1977, the lighthouse was decommissioned and passed to the National Park Service. (United States Coast Guard.)

Beverly's Hospital Point Light took its name from a geographical location named for an early-19th-century smallpox hospital. The light was constructed in 1872 as a singular aid to navigation, but in 1927, it was joined by another. That year, the steeple of the First Baptist Church in Beverly was fitted with a light that, when lined up with the light at Hospital Point, assured safe passage into Salem Harbor. The Coast Guard converted the keeper's home to bunk 20 men during World War II, then automated the light in 1947. In 2009, the Coast Guard signed a memorandum of agreement with a local Coast Guard Auxiliary unit that will allow the public greater access to the lighthouse via guided tours. The lighthouse and quarters have also served as private housing for the commander of the First Coast Guard District. (United States Coast Guard.)

One of the most obvious features of the Nahant landscape, the Nahant Coast Guard Station, opened in 1900 and served boaters from Revere to Swampscott and beyond. It closed in 1963, despite 157 rescue operations that year. Besides its long history of search and rescue operations, the station is also noteworthy for its radio history. The Coast Guard's first Main Radio Traffic station (later Primary Radio station) was commissioned here on October 6, 1926, under the call sign NCP, yet another weapon the Coast Guard planned to use in the war on "demon rum." The radio station—a transmitter, receiver, and four men—closed in 1930, when the Coast Guard negotiated space at Winthrop's Fort Heath. Restoration and reuse plans for the Nahant Coast Guard Station are ongoing. The building stands today as an important reminder of the Coast Guard's role as a protector of the North Shore. (United States Coast Guard.)

Two

BOSTON HARBOR AND THE SOUTH SHORE

Base Boston has long served as the nerve center of the Coast Guard in New England. Today, a small boat station shares space at the 427 Commercial Street facility, now known as Integrated Services Command (ISC) Boston, with cutters, an Aids to Navigation (ATON) team, a marine safety office (MSO), and more. Times change, however. On the left side of this image, the *Cross Rip* lightship awaits orders. Today, there are no active lightships in the United States. (United States Coast Guard.)

Boston Harbor history resounds with tales of Coast Guard heroism. From the beginning of the Colonial era, the complicated series of channels through the harbor's more than 30 islands called for numerous lighthouses, many of which came and went before the Coast Guard era. Deep in the harbor, at City Point in Dorchester, one of the service's two floating stations was built in response to increased recreational boating. It served the people of the harbor into the late 1930s. (United States Coast Guard.)

The first lighthouse in the New World, Boston Light, illuminated the darkness for the first time in 1716. Destroyed during the American Revolution, the old tower gave way to the current structure in 1783, making Boston Light the oldest light station, but not the oldest lighthouse, in the United States. The Coast Guard razed the duplex keeper's house pictured here in the spring of 1960. Today, a civilian keeper, Sally Snowman, stands watch over this ancient lighthouse site. (United States Coast Guard.)

Graves Light, lit on September 1, 1905, represented remote duty for Coast Guardsmen protecting the waterways of Massachusetts. Situated on the rocks that gave the lighthouse its name, Graves lit the way into Boston's northern channel. Coast Guardsmen served at Graves until automation in 1976, evacuating at least once due to a mercury spill in the light. The walkway has been damaged during storms, and the oil house was washed away during the Perfect Storm of 1991. (United States Coast Guard.)

Six miles east of the city and rocking back and forth on an anchor, the Boston Lightship marked the approach to the harbor. Lightship duty was often monotonous and dull, occasionally terrifying, and sometimes deadly. Five different lightships marked the Boston Lightship station during the Coast Guard era. The last lightship, WLV 189, left in 1975 and is now an artificial reef off the New Jersey coast. (Trayser Museum.)

Lightship duty represented some of the loneliest hours any Coast Guardsman could spend in the service. While lighthouses offered remote locations and near solitude, they usually boasted at least some surrounding land. Lightship sailors had nowhere to go but elsewhere on their small ships. Local men such as Pat Reed, shown here at the Cohasset Country Club, did their best to ease the boredom of those men. (United States Coast Guard.)

For 15 years prior to his death in 1942, James Dean, a former president of the Boston Stock Exchange, carried Boston's Sunday newspapers to the Boston Lightship sailors whenever the weather allowed between April and September. His will stated that the tradition should continue after his passing, marking $10,000 for that purpose. Pat Reed (pictured in his 22-foot lobster boat *Shag*) and others took up the delivery route, making the hour-long run. (United States Coast Guard.)

The Point Allerton Coast Guard Station in Hull, a peninsula jutting northward into Boston Harbor, provided one of the Coast Guard's most decorated heroes, Joshua James, with a working home. Despite its high profile within the service, including its one-time designation as the headquarters of Group Boston (the service has since switched from "groups" to "sectors"), Point Allerton missed out on the 1930s construction wave that upgraded facilities across the country. (United States Coast Guard.)

The Coast Guard did consider purchasing land behind the old station on Gallops Hill in the 1930s, but plans were never finalized, and the crew continued to operate out of the 1889 Life-Saving Service station into the 1960s. Finally, at the end of that decade, the service built and opened its new station farther west, near Pemberton Point, where a boathouse had been in use since the second decade of the 20th century. (United States Coast Guard.)

A marvel of engineering for its time, Minot's Lighthouse off the Cohasset and Scituate shore has stood firm over the rocky ledges for which the area is famous since 1860. Coast Guardsmen spent relatively little time there; it was automated in 1947. Still, as an important aid to navigation, it has required maintenance. Shown in 1989, the tower underwent major repairs, with some of the upper granite blocks being replaced after the lantern room and lens had been flown to shore by helicopter for repairs. (United States Coast Guard.)

Scituate boasted two Life-Saving Service stations that briefly served the Coast Guard after the Life-Saving Service and Revenue Cutter Service merger in 1915. The North Scituate station, standing today as a private residence on Surfside Road, remained active into the 1930s, when a new station opened in Scituate Harbor. (United States Coast Guard.)

The Fourth Cliff station, on the Humarock peninsula, lasted but a brief time. It burned down in 1919. Considering its location at the entrance to the North River and its many tributaries, how might the history of the town have changed had the station been active during Prohibition? (Dick Boonisar.)

Built in the classic Colonial Revival style of the Roosevelt-type stations constructed by the Coast Guard in the 1930s, the new Scituate station opened for operations in 1936. Positioned on First Cliff, the station held room for as many as 40 men at the height of World War II and offered quick access to busy Scituate Harbor, the mouth of the North River to the south, and the rocky ledges marked by Minot's Light to the north. (United States Coast Guard.)

A four-bay garage behind the station with a finished second floor took care of vehicular needs for the crew, while a three-bay boathouse at the end of Sunset Road, also with a finished second floor, allowed for versatile emergency responses. Tied up at the end of the pier, a 40-foot utility boat awaits action. (Trayser Museum.)

Well into the motorized lifeboat era, Coast Guardsmen kept up their rowing skills. Here, the Scituate station's crew prepares to "splash" in their Monomoy lifeboat for rowing practice. (United States Coast Guard.)

A disastrous fire in 1984 damaged the upper portions of the Scituate Coast Guard Station, including the historic cupola. The service restored the building, including a pair of pavilions bookending the main house, and operated it into the 1990s. Federal budget cuts resulting in "right-sizing" led to the designation of Scituate as a station-small under Point Allerton, at which point the service deemed the building too large for its purposes. While a new station was built across the harbor, the National Oceanic and Atmospheric Administration's Stellwagen Bank National Marine Sanctuary moved into the building, giving it a new lease on life. (United States Coast Guard.)

Farther south, along what was once known as the esplanade of Marshfield's Brant Rock neighborhood, another ancient Life-Saving Service station served well into the Coast Guard era. (United States Coast Guard.)

Coast Guardsmen of the World War II era and beyond maintained the ancient traditions of lifeboat drills performed by their occupational ancestors of the Life-Saving Service. Capsizing and recovery could mean life and death, not only for marine disaster victims, but for the Coast Guardsmen, as well. (Dick Boonisar.)

The Coast Guard began heavily monitoring radio traffic during Prohibition, setting up a shore radio station in Nahant in 1926. The station moved to Fort Heath in Winthrop in 1931, until it was reclaimed by the Army in 1939. Radio communications then moved to Truro. In 1942, the Coast Guard took 65 acres in Marshfield by eminent domain, converting a mansion (upper left) into offices, barracks, and a mess, and building the rest of the facilities needed to begin "pounding brass" under the call sign NMF. (United States Coast Guard.)

Communication Station Boston, as it would eventually be called, took over the duties of Radio Station New York in 1972. By 1975, Marshfield could no longer contain the station, and all transmitter facilities were moved to the Otis Air National Guard Base on Cape Cod while new receiving facilities were built locally. At its height, under the motto "No Call Unanswered," Communication Station Boston handled 30,000 messages per month. Today, the Marshfield site is open space utilized by the town recreation department. (United States Coast Guard.)

The entryway to Plymouth Harbor rested securely under the watchful eyes of Coast Guardsmen at Plymouth, or Gurnet Light; Duxbury Pier, or Bug Light; and the Gurnet Coast Guard Station. Plymouth Light, pictured prior to 1962, once had a twin, the foundation of which can be seen directly to the right of the tower. The lighthouse and its attendant buildings, as well as the army observation tower to the left, sat on the grounds of the Revolution's Fort Andrew. (United States Coast Guard.)

In 1962, the Coast Guard removed the two-story keeper's house to make room for the new dwelling pictured here. Despite local protests, the lighthouse was automated in 1986. Just over a decade later, encroaching erosion forced a move, as contractors moved the lighthouse 140 feet. Today, a nonprofit organization oversees the lighthouse and rents the keeper's dwelling out to interested parties. (United States Coast Guard.)

The Gurnet Coast Guard Station reached back to the earliest days of the United States Life-Saving Service in Massachusetts. The first building, constructed in 1874, gave way to the Bibb #2-type station pictured, which was built in 1892. (United States Coast Guard.)

A launchway built in 1907 eased the burden on the Life-Saving crew then working at the Gurnet, giving them a 92-foot run to the sea from their boathouse. In 1917, the Commandant of the Coast Guard, Ellsworth P. Bertholf, argued for the erection of a new boathouse to be located 1.5 miles away on Saquish Head, citing ice problems in winter. The General Services Administration accepted the station property in 1957 and sold it at auction in 1968. (United States Coast Guard.)

Deep inside Massachusetts Bay, the first Manomet Point Life-Saving Station opened its doors in 1874. At that time, its primary role was to protect coastwise shipping moving between Barnstable Harbor and the South Shore. Things would soon change, however. A new station building, constructed in 1901 in the Duluth-type architectural style notable for its tall observation tower, supplanted the old building. The Cape Cod Canal opened to the south 13 years later, diverting marine traffic that once passed around the outer bended arm of Cape Cod to the waters directly in front of the Manomet Point station, which the following year would be relabeled a Coast Guard station. The station opened an auxiliary boathouse on the canal to better watch over the ever-increasing traffic. (National Archives and Records Administration.)

That auxiliary boathouse, near the eastern end of the canal, would eventually grow into a thriving unit all its own. As the search and rescue game changed in the first half of the 20th century because of larger ships with more carrying capacity and therefore fewer commercial vessels on the water, better propulsion systems for those ships, the rise of motor lifeboats, and increases in communications technology, most of the early lifesaving stations closed on the South Shore. (Dick Boonisar.)

As the new Cape Cod Canal station arose in 1936, so did the station in Scituate. Point Allerton remained in service, but North Scituate, Brant Rock, Gurnet, and Manomet Point teetered on the precipice of permanent closure. World War II extended their usefulness for a few more years, but by the 1950s, the new picture of the Coast Guard on the South Shore came into focus. (United States Coast Guard.)

Any stretch of coastline holds its share of wild tales, and the South Shore is no different. Fantastical rescue stories from Boston Harbor to the Cape Cod Canal stand their ground against tales told elsewhere. Rumrunners had their heyday on the South Shore, and the Coast Guard, as the enforcing agency behind the Volstead Act, was for the first time forced into the role of bad guy with the American public. Not even the hallowed grounds of Plymouth were free from smugglers. Here, a Coast Guard crew from Scituate brings their 38-foot picket boat (left) in view of the Plymouth Rock portico to inspect suspected rummies. The Coast Guard's small-boat crews have always done amazing things, but there have been times when larger vessels and bigger crews have been required to effect rescues. At those times, the Coast Guard calls upon its bigger vessels, the cutters. (Dick Boonisar.)

Three

THE CUTTERS

The *Bear*, the most famous of all Coast Guard cutters, was built in 1874 for sealing in Newfoundland. It was acquired in 1884 by the US Navy to search for the Greely Arctic expedition. In 1885, she became commissioned as a Revenue Cutter and in 1929, as a Coast Guard Cutter. She had a legendary 41-year career in Alaskan waters. The *Bear* came to Boston in 1932, and in 1933 and 1939, she sailed from Boston to Antarctica as part of Adm. Richard E. Byrd's second Antarctic expedition. She was lost to the sea while being towed from Nova Scotia to Philadelphia in 1963. (United States Coast Guard.)

Because of their availability and speed (29-plus knots), Navy destroyers were thought a good fit for the Rum Patrol. The *Paulding* was built in 1910, the first of its class, and served in World War I escorting convoys. She was transferred in 1924 to the Coast Guard and stationed in Boston. During a gale on December 17, 1927, while searching for another Coast Guard cutter, the *Paulding* rammed Navy submarine *S-4* off Provincetown as it was surfacing. The submarine sank and the crew was lost. The Coast Guard was absolved of blame for the sinking. (United States Coast Guard.)

The *Faunce*, an Active-class patrol boat was built in 1927. She was stationed in Boston for the length of her service. In World War II, she saw duty on the Greenland Patrol. She escorted convoys and did patrol work. This class of cutters gave long service. Some of them were in service through the 1960s. The *Faunce* was decommissioned in 1948. (United States Coast Guard.)

The *Chelan*, a Lake-class cutter, was built in 1928 in Quincy, Massachusetts, by the Bethlehem Shipbuilding Corporation. She was assigned to Boston in 1937. On March 22, 1937, she rescued the crew of the sinking Norwegian ship *Bjerkli*. A gale was blowing from the northwest, and the seas were high. When the *Chelan* reached the *Bjerkli*, she was low in the water and in danger of sinking. The crew of the *Bjerkli* was taken aboard, the steamer sank, and the *Chelan* headed to Boston, 660 miles away. (United States Coast Guard.)

The *Marion*, an Active-class patrol boat, was built in 1927. In this photograph, taken on July 11, 1928, she is leaving Boston on an oceanographic research mission to Baffin Bay and the Davis Strait, located between Greenland and Canada's Baffin Island. The cutter and the expedition were commanded by LCDR Edward H. "Iceberg" Smith. The 8,100-mile expedition established the origin and predictability of icebergs. Smith achieved the rank of rear admiral, earned a PhD, and was appointed director of the Oceanographic Institution at Woods Hole, Massachusetts. (United States Coast Guard.)

The *Humboldt*, a Casco-class cutter, was built in the Boston Naval Shipyard in 1941 as a seaplane tender. In 1949, she was transferred to the Coast Guard. She was stationed in Boston from March 1949 to September 1966. Her duties were law enforcement, weather stations, and search and rescue operations. In 1966, she was transferred to Portland, Maine. During her stay in Maine, she rescued the crew of the sailing vessel *Atlantic* on October 29, 1968. (United States Coast Guard.)

The *Natsek* was built as the wooden fishing trawler *Belmont*. The Coast Guard acquired her and commissioned her on June 19, 1942. She was assigned to the commander in chief of Atlantic Command (CINCLANT) and the Greenland Patrol. The *Natsek* was lost with all hands while returning from Greenland sometime around December 17, 1942. This happened in the vicinity of Newfoundland, and the cause unknown. She is pictured in Boston Harbor. (United States Coast Guard.)

The *Active* was built in 1927 as the first of her class of patrol boats. From 1942 to 1945, she was home ported in Boston while serving on the Greenland Patrol. In 1946, after a short time being stationed in Miami, she was again stationed in Boston, but she was out of service because of a shortage of personnel. The *Active* was moved to California in the 1950s and was decommissioned in 1962. (United States Coast Guard.)

The *Northland* was built in 1927. She was designed for Arctic operations, with auxiliary sails that were removed in 1936. In 1939, she came to Boston to take part in Byrd's second Antarctic expedition. The expedition was canceled because of war in Europe. In 1940, she became part of Comdr. Edward "Iceberg" Smith's Greenland Survey project. Greenland was strategically important to the United States, as it was the largest source of cryolite, a mineral used in extracting aluminum from alumina. (United States Coast Guard.)

The *Northland* carried a seaplane in 1941, an SOC-4 Curtiss Seagull. In 1942, the seaplane was replaced with a J2F-5 Grumman Duck. The Greenland Patrol had two divisions. The South Greenland Patrol consisted of cutters *Modoc, Comanche, Raritan,* and the *Bowdoin,* a former Coast and Geodetic Survey vessel. The North Greenland Patrol consisted of cutters *Northland, Bear,* and *North Star,* which was a former Department of the Interior vessel. (United States Coast Guard.)

In July 1944, the cutter *Northland* discovered the German trawler *Coburg*. This is one of the ships the Germans were using to establish a presence in Greenland. The trawler had been stuck in the ice and destroyed by fire by her crew. *Northland* had already destroyed a German weather station at Cape Sussie, Greenland. (United States Coast Guard.)

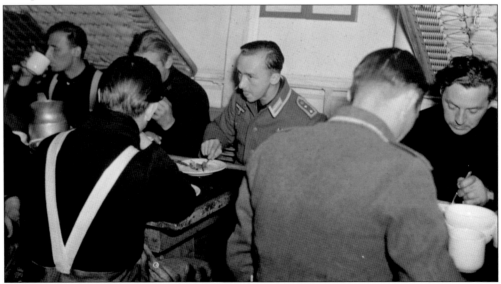

In September 1944, the *Northland* discovered another German vessel at sea and pursued it for 70 miles in icy waters off Great Koldewey Island. The Germans surrendered and scuttled their ship. The photograph shows some of the German prisoners enjoying Coast Guard hospitality below deck on the *Northland*. In 1946, the *Northland* was decommissioned and sold. In 1947, she was named *The Jewish State*. She transported Jewish immigrants past the British blockade to Palestine. After 1948, she became the first Israeli warship and fought against Egyptian naval forces. (United States Coast Guard.)

The *Eastwind* was built in 1943 as a Wind-class cutter modeled after the Swedish icebreaker *Yrner*. During World War II, she was stationed in Boston and operated in Greenland waters. Under the command of Capt. Charles W. Thomas, a German weather station was captured on October 4, 1944. The armed German trawler *Externsteine* and its crew of 17 were captured on October 15, 1944. After the war, *Eastwind* returned to Boston. She made many trips to the Arctic and Antarctic. She was decommissioned in 1968 and scrapped in 1972. (United States Coast Guard.)

On his Greenland Patrol in October 1944, Captain Thomas of the *Eastwind* searched for likely locations of German weather stations. He sent the ship's seaplane in search of unusual activities. They spotted a vessel that could have been a German trawler and they also saw a possible encampment on North Little Koldewey Island. The captain ordered a landing of a specially trained force to capture the encampment. On October 4, 1944, they captured 12 men, supplies, and information about three other German expeditions. (United States Coast Guard.)

This is the German Navy's vessel SNS *Externsteine*, captured October 15, 1944. The *Eastwind's* plane spotted the ship stuck in the ice east of Greenland's Cape Borgen. Captain Thomas wanted to capture the ship intact and the crew alive. The plan was to use a display of firepower to surprise and frighten the German crew into surrendering without damaging their ship. His plan, which included the *Southwind*, worked. The only enemy surface vessel captured during the war was renamed the *Eastbreeze* and was sent to Boston and given to the Navy, which named it USS *Callao*. (United States Coast Guard.)

The *North Star* was built in 1932 for the Department of the Interior in Seattle, Washington. The Coast Guard took her over in 1941 and assigned her to the Northeast Greenland Patrol out of Boston. She participated, along with the *Bear* and *Northland*, in the capture of the Norwegian trawler *Buskoe*. This ship was serving German weather stations in Greenland. The trawler and her crew were sent to Boston for internment. (United States Coast Guard.)

The *Sea Cloud* was built in 1931 in Kiel, Germany, for E.F. Hutton. For several years, she was commissioned alternately by the Navy and the Coast Guard, where she was used as a weather ship, and home ported in Boston. In 1944, Lt. Carlton Skinner proposed a plan for racial integration. Under his command, African Americans were allowed to train in ratings other than steward's mate. Taking part in the training, which proved to be a success, were 50 seamen and two officers. (United States Coast Guard.)

The *Menemsha* was built as the *Lake Orange* in 1918. She was acquired by the Navy in 1941 and converted from a lake cargo hauler to a weather patrol ship. She was loaned to the Coast Guard in 1942 and commissioned by the Coast Guard in 1943. While on weather patrols from Boston, she had many run-ins with U-boats. While patrolling south of Newfoundland on August 20, 1942, she rescued five survivors from the British ship *Arlett*, torpedoed by *U-458*. (United States Coast Guard.)

The *Campbell* was built in 1936 as a Treasury-class cutter. Boston became the *Campbell*'s homeport on February 18, 1942. On February 22, 1943, as the *Campbell* was returning to its convoy after assisting a torpedoed tanker, she spotted a U-boat (*U-606*). As the *Campbell* attacked, the submarine's bow plane sliced the *Campbell*'s hull, flooding the engine room. The submarine was sunk. The *Campbell* picked up five of the U-boat survivors and was towed to St. John's, Newfoundland. (United States Coast Guard.)

In 1945, the *Campbell* was shifted to the Pacific. In 1946, she was stationed out of Brooklyn, New York. She was back in Massachusetts waters to assist in the rescue effort during the *Andrea Doria* and *Stockholm* collision in 1956. In 1959, she was in the Greenland ice fields directing a seven day search for *Han Hedtoft*, a Danish ship that was lost after hitting an iceberg. No survivors were found. The *Campbell* served in Vietnam in 1968. She was decommissioned in 1982 and sunk as a target ship in 1984. (Paul Rooney.)

The *Spencer* was built in 1937 as a Secretary-class cutter. She was assigned to the Neutrality Patrols in 1939 under the command of the Boston District. Much of her history was spent in the battle of the Atlantic. During World War II, *Spencer* was on convoy escort duty out of Boston and other ports. In 1946, after the war, *Spencer* was home ported in Boston until 1947. In 1969, she went back to war in Vietnam. She was decommissioned in 1974, sold, and scrapped. (United States Coast Guard.)

This photograph of the *Spencer* was taken from the cutter *Duane* while escorting convoy HX-233 in April 1943 from New York. Two combat photographers were on board, Jack January on the *Spencer* and Bob Gates on the *Duane*. This convoy had 57 merchant ships and was escorted by Escort Group A3, which included the two cutters, one destroyer, and six corvettes from Britain and Canada. On April 15, U-boats began approaching the convoy. On April 17, the *Spencer* made contact with *U-175* and began to attack with depth charges. (United States Coast Guard.)

U-175 has been damaged by Spencer's depth charge attack and is forced to the surface in this image. Note the German sailor standing aft of the conning tower. The cutter *Duane* has come to assist, and nearby merchant ships are firing on the submarine. This U-boat is a type IXC submarine. She made three patrols and sank 10 Allied ships. There were 13 German sailors killed; the *Spencer* picked up 19 and the *Duane* picked up 22. (United States Coast Guard.)

The *Spencer* crew at first thought they might be able to capture *U-175* or at least be able to retrieve important information or equipment from the submarine. A boat was lowered with a boarding party. They did manage to get aboard the submarine, but it began to sink. The German crew had opened the dive valves as they abandoned ship. (United States Coast Guard.)

For these German *U-175* men, the war is over. They were pulled from the Atlantic, given food, a change of clothes, and medical attention. They enjoyed Coast Guard hospitality all the way to Scotland, where they were transferred to a prisoner of war camp. There are lots of smiles for these men, as they are the lucky ones. U-boat crews nicknamed their submarines iron coffins. (United States Coast Guard.)

The *Duane* was built in 1936 as a Secretary-class cutter. In 1939, its home port was Boston. On February 22, 1942, the *Duane* was on convoy duty. Lt. Robert W. Goehring was inspecting a gun when a large wave hit the quarterdeck and washed him over the side. The man-overboard alarm was sounded and the cutter turned. As the cutter came alongside Goehring, a wave lifted him to the height of the deck and crew members were able to pull him aboard. (United States Coast Guard.)

On March 15, 1983, 270 miles off Delaware Bay, the *Duane* intercepted a suspicious coastal freighter, the *Civinney*, which was registered in Honduras. The *Civinney* denied a consensual boarding. The *Duane* had to wait for boarding permission from officials. The next morning, the crew of the *Civinney* set her on fire and opened the sea cocks. The crew abandoned their ship in the lifeboat seen in this photograph. (United States Coast Guard.)

The *Duane's* crew fought the fire and tried to stop the flooding, but the *Civinney* sank. The crew was arrested and brought to Cape May, New Jersey. A full 60 tons of marijuana were on board. In July 1985, the *Duane* participated in the Boston Harborfest, and in August, she was decommissioned. She was the oldest warship in the United States and the queen of the fleet. She was sunk along with the cutter *Bibb* in 1987 as an artificial reef off Molasses Reef in Key Largo, Florida. (United States Coast Guard.)

The *Escanaba* was built in 1932 as an A-class cutter. She was home ported in Boston in 1942. Lt. Robert Prause, executive officer of the *Escanaba*, developed the rescue swimmer system, which had a swimmer in a wetsuit tie a line to the victim. The line was then used to pull the victim on board. On February 3, 1943, the transport USAT *Dorchester* was torpedoed and sunk. The *Escanaba* saved 133 men. On June 10, 1943, the *Escanaba* was sunk, and there were only two survivors. The exact cause of the sinking is unknown. (United States Coast Guard.)

In 1946, a new cutter of the Owasco class was named *Escanaba*. She was home ported in New Bedford from 1957 to 1973. She assisted the US MV *American Pilot* and the *Maumee* following their collision west of the Cape Cod Canal, November 1965. She rescued two survivors from the MV *Monte Palomares*, which sank in heavy seas with a loss of 31 crew members on January 10, 1966. She was decommissioned in 1974 and scrapped. (United States Coast Guard.)

The *Casco* was built in 1941 for the Navy as a seaplane tender. She was commissioned by the Coast Guard in 1949. Her home port was Boston for her entire service. As part of the various duties, she fought a fire on March 27, 1968, on Long Wharf in Boston. The original caption on this photograph reads, in part, "(1-23-69) Escorted by a plane . . . *Casco* departs Boston, Mass. to make her last . . . weather patrol." She was decommissioned in 1969 and returned to the Navy, where she was used as a target. (United States Coast Guard.)

The *General Greene* was built in 1927 as an Active-class patrol boat. She was home ported in Boston in 1927. In the 1930s, she was moved to Woods Hole. In 1941, off Newfoundland, she searched for survivors of two British ships that were torpedoed off Greenland. She rescued 39 crew members from the freighter SS *Marconi*. While on this mission, she witnessed the battle of the *Bismarck*. On May 25, 1942, she rescued 18 survivors from the torpedoed British ship SS *Peisander* off Nantucket Shoals. (Paul Rooney.)

In 1947, the *General Greene* was moved from Woods Hole to Gloucester. On March 6, 1960, on a rescue mission off East Sandwich, she grounded when her tow line became entangled in her propellers; she lost power, and her anchors would not hold. It took four days, with the help of the cutter *Acushnet* and the Massachusetts National Guard, to refloat her. She was decommissioned in 1968 and sold in 1976. Registered in Guatemala as the *Belmont*, she was seized for smuggling drugs. (Dick Boonisar.)

The *Taney*, a Secretary-class cutter, was built in 1939. The *Taney* came to Boston from Honolulu in 1943. She worked escorting conveys. In October 1944, she was in the Charlestown Navy Yard to be converted into an amphibious command ship with accommodations for a flag officer and his staff. Today, *Taney* is the last US warship afloat that was at Pearl Harbor on December 7, 1941. She now serves a museum ship in Baltimore, Maryland. (United States Coast Guard.)

The *McCulloch*, a Casco-class cutter, was built in 1946. She was home ported in Boston from 1946 to 1966. She was assigned to the Cuban Patrol during the Cuban Exodus of 1965 and rescued 280 Cubans from small craft in the Florida Straits. The *McCulloch* was transferred to the Republic of Vietnam and named *Ngo Kuyen*. After the fall of Saigon, the she sailed to the Philippines. Reacquired by the United States, she was given to the Philippine navy and named RPS#8 *Gregorio*. She served until 1990. (United States Coast Guard.)

Four

THE SOUTH COAST
AND THE ISLANDS

Massachusetts provided the western world with its first form of currency when the local Native Americans began trading wampum with European visitors on what would become the South Coast. Seagoing commerce has ever since been a way of life for New Bedford, Fall River, the towns of Buzzards Bay, and Martha's Vineyard, Nantucket, and the Elizabeth Islands. The Coast Guard, under its old motto to "save lives and property," has therefore seen the region as important to its mission. The first Revenue Cutter School of Instruction, the forerunner to today's Coast Guard Academy, opened near New Bedford in 1876. (United States Coast Guard.)

Even prior to the establishment of the United States, as seen at Boston Lighthouse in Boston Harbor, lighthouses became the primary manifestation of the country's willingness to protect its commercial interests. The sparkplug-style Butler Flats Lighthouse first lit up the New Bedford shoreline in 1898 and was automated in 1978. Coast Guardsman Henry Sieg, one of the station's two crewman, rescued three people from a capsized sailboat when he rowed to their rescue in 1975. (United States Coast Guard.)

Perhaps one of the most tragic tales in Coast Guard history centers on New Bedford's Palmer's Island Lighthouse and the Hurricane of 1938. The storm struck the South Coast the year before the Coast Guard took control of the nation's lighthouses, and it claimed the life Mabel Small, the wife of lighthouse keeper Arthur Small. The light was automated in 1941. (United States Coast Guard.)

Slammed by the Hurricane of 1938, Fall River's Borden Flats Lighthouse lists slightly. The wide base seen in this photograph was an addition after the hurricane, which hopefully offered the remote lighthouse more protection from the sea. Lit in 1881, the light was electrified in 1957 and automated six years later. During periods of heavy fog, local residents listen for the foghorn every 10 seconds. (United States Coast Guard.)

The Coast Guard home ported cutters in New Bedford for most of the 20th century. The cutter *Yakutat*, the large cutter tied to the dock, served the region from 1949 to 1971. Her final years in service to the country were spent in Vietnam. The last cutters to leave New Bedford did so in 2003. In November 2010, the mayor of the "Whaling City" made a plea for the Coast Guard to return. (United States Coast Guard.)

Mattapoisett's Ned's Point Lighthouse continues to shine today. Its operation was interrupted only briefly, between the Coast Guard's deactivation of the lighthouse in 1952 and the town's relighting of it in 1961 as part of a beautiful new public park. (United States Coast Guard.)

The lighthouse at Wing's Neck in Bourne, across Buzzards Bay, shares a bit of history with Ned's Point. In 1923, the wooden keeper's dwelling at Ned's Point was deemed expendable to that station's interests. It was placed on a barge and relocated to Wing's Neck. Just 22 years later, the light at Wing's Neck was deactivated. Its heyday coincided with the opening of the Cape Cod Canal in 1914, as its position made it the perfect place from which to monitor traffic into the new waterway. (United States Coast Guard.)

The reason Wing's Neck lost its position of prominence was due to the construction of the new Cleveland East Ledge Lighthouse in 1941. The cutter *Arbutus* is shown during the building of the light. Massachusetts began the process, then handed it off to the Coast Guard, making it the only lighthouse in the state built by the service. Due to delays fostered by the onset of World War II, the light was not active until 1943. (United States Coast Guard.)

From 1954 to 1961, lightship sailors wearing Coast Guard blues guarded the entrance to Buzzards Bay aboard LV 86 (1954–1959) and LV 110 (1959–1961). The latter vessel is shown here. In 1961, the lightship steamed off station to make way for the new offshore Buzzards Bay Entrance Light. The lightship itself had replaced the Vineyard Sound and Hens and Chickens lightships. (United States Coast Guard.)

Some traditions die hard. When the Coast Guard took command of the nation's lighthouses in 1939, keepers then on the payroll of the predecessor agency were given the option to remain civilians or join the service. Joseph Hindley decided to retain his civilian status throughout his service to lighthouses and finally retired from Nobska Point in 1973. Only then did uniformed Coast Guard personnel take up positions at this famed Falmouth lighthouse. (United States Coast Guard.)

The Coast Guard's history in Woods Hole reaches back to 1857, when the Lighthouse Service purchased land there for a maintenance depot. The Revenue Cutter Service cutter *Acushnet*, shown here, was already posted to Woods Hole when that service merged with the Life-Saving Service in 1915 to become the Coast Guard. (United States Coast Guard.)

The land at Woods Hole, on Little Harbor, served the Lighthouse Service well as a place where buoys and other aids to navigation could be prepared, repaired, painted, and put into service. The site transformed from Base Woods Hole to the headquarters of Group Woods Hole when the Coast Guard took on that classification system for its regions. It's now known as the headquarters of Sector Southern New England. (Trayser Museum.)

Sector Southern New England formed through the merging of Group Woods Hole and Marine Safety Office, Providence, Rhode Island. It oversees eight small-boat rescue stations, four cutters, two aids to navigation teams, and the marine safety office, with detachments of the latter in Bourne and New Bedford. The Coast Guard's presence in the area has lasted more than 150 years. (United States Coast Guard.)

The small lighthouse at Tarpaulin Cove on Naushon Island was automated in 1941, shortly after the Coast Guard's absorption of the Lighthouse Service. The cove, on the largest of the Elizabeth Islands, boasts pirate legends. It got its name from the notion that ships hauled in there to cover their goods with waterproof, tar-covered palls, a process known as tarpalling or tarpawling. (United States Coast Guard.)

Little Cuttyhunk Island, at the seaward end of the island chain, held both a lifesaving station and a lighthouse. It also has the distinction of being located next to a leper colony, which operated on nearby Penikese Island. In 1937, the Coast Guard built a new station to replace the old station, and then replaced this one in the 1960s. Here, the first and second buildings stand during the short transition period. (United States Coast Guard.)

If the Menemsha station looks familiar, there are two reasons. First, it is built in the standard style of the 1930s Coast Guard's building program. Second, it is the old Cuttyhunk station. In 1952, the service floated the station to Martha's Vineyard to replace the old Gay Head Lifesaving Station, though it retained the name Cuttyhunk for the next 20 years. The boathouse at Menemsha, built in 1939 to replace the one destroyed by the Hurricane of 1938, was lost to fire in July 2010. (United States Coast Guard.)

For a short period, Martha's Vineyard, specifically Gay Head (now Aquinnah), hosted a long range navigation (LORAN) site. Constructed in August 1957, the Vineyard site tracked ships at sea using low frequency radio transmitters. By 1962, the Vineyard's association with LORAN was over, as the station transferred to Nantucket. (United States Coast Guard.)

Near some of the New World's busiest shipping centers, Martha's Vineyard witnessed numerous major shipwrecks during its first four centuries of European settlement. Vineyard Sound, in particular, could be particularly treacherous. From 1847 until 1954, lightships known either as Vineyard Sound or Sow and Pigs (for the rocks so named in the area) helped guide ships through the area. Lightship 110, shown here, later became the Buzzards Bay lightship. (United States Coast Guard.)

The Hens and Chickens, Sow and Pigs, and Bishop and Clerks themes for lightship names occurred wherever one large rock seemingly had a court of smaller rocks surrounding it. The Hens and Chickens light station, two miles south of Westport's Horseneck Beach, existed nearly as long as its Vineyard Sound counterpart, from 1866 to 1954, when it, too, was replaced by the Buzzards Bay station. (United States Coast Guard.)

Gay Head Light began service in 1799 with a tower that no longer stands. The current tower, built in 1854, was one of the first in the United States to receive a Fresnel lens, the light capturing and refracting mechanism that would stay in commission for most of the next century and a half. The Gay Head Fresnel was replaced in 1952, at which time the lens transferred to the Dukes County (now Martha's Vineyard) Historical Society. The keeper's dwelling seen here was torn down in 1956. (United States Coast Guard.)

Chappaquiddick's Cape Poge Light shares the island with Gay Head, Edgartown Harbor Light, and the East and West Chop Lighthouses, bracketing Vineyard Haven Harbor. Erosion forced Cape Poge Light inland in 1893. The new light was constructed 40 feet from the original. It was moved in 1907, 1922, 1960, and here, in 1986. Despite automation during World War II, the light remains a going concern for both the Coast Guard and the people of Martha's Vineyard. (United States Coast Guard.)

Nantucket's Coast Guard nerve center today sits at Brant Point, but that concentration of activity belies the island-wide connection between Nantucket and the Coast Guard. During the Life-Saving Service era, Nantucketers served at stations at Coskata, Maddaket, Muskeget, and Surfside. (United States Coast Guard.)

Lighthouses have long been part of the Nantucket landscape as well. The first Great Point Lighthouse, on the northeastern tip of the island, was built in 1785 but lost to fire in 1816. The second tower rose in 1818 but fell prey to a horrific storm in March 1984. Sen. Ted Kennedy fought for appropriations to rebuild the light and raised the flag in dedication on September 7, 1986. (United States Coast Guard.)

Siasconset's Sankaty Head Lighthouse was manned by Coast Guard personnel until 1992, although the light had been automated in 1965. Threatened by erosion, the light was moved in 2007 in a major undertaking that pulled it to a distance of 250 feet from the edge of the cliff. (United States Coast Guard.)

Satellite maps of Nantucket today show a perfect circle on the southeastern corner of the island, the site of the Nantucket LORAN station. Established in 1943, the station eventually absorbed the Martha's Vineyard station and served sailors into the 21st century. In 2010, the Coast Guard ceased operations of all LORAN stations, finding that the global positioning system to have made the LORAN system redundant. (United States Coast Guard.)

The words cross and rip, when used in conjunction, are plenty to make any sailor sit up and take notice. The lightship bearing the name steered mariners between Cross Rip Shoal and Horseshoe Shoal in Nantucket Sound between 1828 and 1963. (United States Coast Guard.)

A glimpse into the interior of the Cross Rip Lightship shows just how Spartan accommodations could be on an American lightship. Much of the space below decks was reserved for the operation of the ship. Whatever space was left went to the galley, the mess, and living quarters. Whatever could be nailed down, was. (United States Coast Guard.)

The Nantucket Shoals Lightship was one of the most exposed, most dangerous lightship stations in US waters. In May 1934, the White Star liner *Olympic* ran down LV 117 in the fog, killing seven members of the lightship crew. Because of its importance as a primary point of contact for ships approaching from Europe, the Nantucket lightship station was the last one decommissioned in the country. Since steaming off station in 1983, the last Nantucket Shoals Lightship, WLV 612 (the "W" signifies Coast Guard construction), has led a tumultuous life, from museum ship to floating office and from Boston to New York. It is currently available for charters, events, and vacation rentals. (United States Coast Guard.)

No mention of the Coast Guard on Nantucket can be complete without the story of "Madaket Millie" Jewett. Born on Nantucket in 1907, Millie began volunteering around the local lifesaving station, according to local legend, at four years old. Removed from the heart of the action at the center of town, her life was the Coast Guard. She aided in rescues, trained service dogs in World War II, and led her own beach patrols. When the local station closed on January 3, 1947, she personally led the race to rescue the crew of the grounded steamer *Kotor*. Later that year, she officially joined the Coast Guard Auxiliary, and in 1952, the Coast Guard named her an honorary warrant officer. That title later grew to commanding officer, West End Command in 1965, but she was not done yet. In 1967, she directed rescue crews to a downed Air Force EC-121H Warning Star. In 1975, she was authorized to fly storm warning flags from her home. She died in 1990 at 82, with more than seven decades of volunteer service to the Coast Guard and a Meritorious Public Service Award attached to her name. (United States Coast Guard.)

Five

CAPE COD

When the Coast Guard opened its new station in Provincetown's West End in 1979, it was not the beginning of a new era. It was, in fact, the continuance of a long-term relationship the service has had with Cape Cod. The new station, the first federal building in US history to use solar power, reconfirmed the service's commitment to the safety of the fishermen of Provincetown and the surrounding communities. (United States Coast Guard.)

Wood End Lighthouse has lit the way for mariners since 1873, unfortunately witnessing one of the Coast Guard's most tragic moments—the 1927 collision between the submarine S-4 and the Coast Guard cutter *Paulding* 1/2 mile away. The Navy acquired the lighthouse from the Coast Guard in 1979 and converted it to solar power two years later. (United States Coast Guard.)

A near mirror image of Wood End, the current Long Point Lighthouse began guiding mariners into Provincetown Harbor in 1875. Long Point was automated in 1952 and Wood Island in 1961. (United States Coast Guard.)

The Race Point Lighthouse's ray first pierced the sky in 1816, the third lighthouse built on Cape Cod. That tower, a stone and mortar creation, fell prey to the disintegrating effects of the ocean's spray by 1875. The following year, a new steel tower that still stands today replaced it. A full 78 years later, electricity reached the light station, making life for the Coast Guardsmen on duty that much easier. The light was automated in 1972. In recent years, the light station, the tower, and all remaining outbuildings have undergone a thorough restoration by a volunteer crew led by Jim Walker of Hyannis. That crew has since moved onto Sandy Neck Lighthouse in Barnstable Harbor, bringing light back to that station. Guarding the northwestern tip of Cape Cod (the balled fist of the bended arm), Race Point Lighthouse remains an active aid to navigation. (United States Coast Guard.)

Wood End also boasted an early lifesaving station. In 1872, the year after the reformation of the United States Life-Saving Service in the aftermath of political debates as to its viability and effectiveness, Cape Cod found itself the unwitting recipient of nine federally funded rescue stations. Provincetown itself had four. This station at Wood End, which lasted into World War II, was built in 1896. (United States Coast Guard.)

The Race Point Coast Guard Station, separate from the lighthouse, served to react to the disasters the lighthouse attempted to prevent. The station remains today, in use by the National Park Service as part of the Cape Cod National Seashore infrastructure. The new station, completed in 1930, was quickly outmoded when it became apparent it would be too distant from its own boats, which increasingly needed dock space rather than a boat room and marine railway. (United States Coast Guard.)

Peaked Hill Bars Sta.

Deep Hollow

Ocean

The precariousness of life on the dunes of Provincetown was borne out by the Peaked Hill Bars Coast Guard Station. Marked historically for the loss of three Life-Saving Service crew members in 1880, the station teetered between the ocean and a hollow in the dunes. The first station on this site briefly became the home of playwright Eugene O'Neill before sliding off the cliff to its doom. The newer station remained active into the late 1930s. Another nearby station, called High Head, watched over the southern end of the Peaked Hill Bars from 1882 to 1921. (United States Coast Guard.)

Mariners approaching Boston Harbor knew they were too far to the south when they could see the lighthouse in North Truro, known as Cape Cod Light. The light station, established in 1797, survives to this day, though with major changes. Automation in 1987 was the least worrisome thing that could have happened. It was the encroachment of the sea that led to the moving of the lighthouse more than 400 feet from the eroding cliffs of the Highlands section of town. The light originally stood 500 feet from the cliffs. Such figures meant nothing to the daily life of the average Coast Guard light keeper. Erosion continues at about three feet per year. (United States Coast Guard.)

The Highland Coast Guard Station was consolidated with the Cape Cod Light Station in 1947 to become the Cape Cod Lifeboat Station. The small crew watched a diminishing caseload and knew what was coming. The station closed in 1952. (United States Coast Guard.)

South of the Highland station, but still in Truro, the crew of the Pamet River Coast Guard Station toiled. Patrols between the stations were near impossible during high tides, especially as erosion ate away at the dunes. Selected as an original Cape Cod site in 1872, Pamet River ceased operations in the 1930s. (United States Coast Guard.)

The problem for such stations came in the various forms of the Life-Saving Service's, and soon thereafter, the Coast Guard's motorized lifeboats. When wooden ships ruled the seas, wooden lifeboats powered by men, covered the coastline; as innovators developed smaller and smaller engines, blood, sweat, and tears were replaced by oil, gas, and grease. Motor lifeboats of 36 feet, like this Type TR lifeboat, heralded the beginning of that era. Boats like the 36-footer and its antecedents, the 44-footer and the modern-day 47-footer, shrunk distances and lessened response times for rescue crews and marine disaster victims. The 36-footer would become synonymous with Cape Cod in the 1950s, and one, the 36500, can still be seen in local waters today. (United States Coast Guard.)

The crew at the Nauset Coast Guard station in Eastham was serving in an older building that proceeded the one pictured when Henry Beston wrote his journal of the natural year on Cape Cod, *The Outermost House*. Beston's only human companionship when he lived at the house were those patrolling from the station. This building, constructed in the 1930s, is now an overnight education center utilized by the National Park Service. (United States Coast Guard.)

Researching Coast Guard history can sometimes be like a puzzle with constantly moving pieces. Nauset Light, shown here, was once one of the twin lights at the Chatham station to the south. In 1923, it replaced the last of the three Nauset lighthouses, known as the Three Sisters of Nauset, all of which are now tucked into the woods just inland of the current lighthouse. (United States Coast Guard.)

The Orleans Coast Guard Station became famous, at least around the Cape, during 1935 for the light-fingered antics of its mascot. A crow, adopted by a surfman at the station, proved to be a thief, stealing milk from the doorsteps of locals and then hightailing it back to the station. One morning, it pilfered a sour bottle and turned up dead. In the lore of the locals, the end came via suicide. (United States Coast Guard.)

The Old Harbor Coast Guard Station started as a Life-Saving Service structure, like so many of the Coast Guard stations on Cape Cod. It still stands today, but not anywhere near its original location north of the Chatham Inlet. In 1977, three decades after the station closed, the National Park Service purchased it and moved it to a spot south of Race Point, where it became part of the interpreted history of the Cape Cod National Seashore. (United States Coast Guard.)

Three other Coast Guard stations graced the Chatham coastline. The Chatham station, shown here in 1937, is now gone, except for the garage. The property was turned over to the US Fish and Wildlife Service in 1955, and that organization still owns and maintains the utility building. (United States Coast Guard.)

Monomoy sported two stations, one part way down the sandy barrier beach (Monomoy) and one at the end (Monomoy Point). In this photograph, the Monomoy Point station is receiving a new garage thanks to the Public Works Administration (PWA), a Depression-era federal program designed to put Americans back to work. (United States Coast Guard.)

One might think that the long uninhabited sandy stretches of the Cape Cod coastline would be perfect for rumrunners, but the Coast Guard learned to think like smugglers and nab them in their tracks. Richard E. Ryder, most likely in Gloucester, displays his catch. Ryder took the helm of four other stations—Monomoy, Chatham, Orleans, and Old Harbor. (Richard Ryder.)

The sandy beaches of Cape Cod called for special equipment from time to time, such as this tractor used to pull the lifeboat to the water's edge, saving both manpower and horsepower. Such innovations led to consolidation in Coast Guard circles in the Chatham area. (United States Coast Guard.)

Ironically, with six station sites to choose from, the Coast Guard opted not to use any of them, instead pooling their resources at the Chatham Lighthouse. This aerial image, taken in 1951, shows LORAN station buildings in the background, behind the main building, which was formerly the keeper's quarters for the lighthouse. (United States Coast Guard.)

As it became apparent that surfmen walking patrols in the sand would be replaced by better communication systems, among other improvements, stations closed. By the early 1950s, the Chatham Lifeboat Station had opened in place of the closing Cahoon's Hollow, Nauset, Old Harbor, Chatham, Monomoy, and Monomoy Point stations. The Morris Island boathouse, shown here in 1951, became increasingly important. (United States Coast Guard.)

Guarding the "elbow" of Cape Cod, the Chatham Lifeboat Station became one of the most famous and storied stations in the United States. Already the lore keepers of the March 1902 Monomoy tragedy, in which all but one member of the local Life-Saving Service crew lost their lives in a rescue attempt, in 1952, Chatham residents witnessed one of the most dramatic rescues in the history of the service when the local crew went to the aid of the T-2 tanker *Pendleton* at the height of a dizzying winter storm. The rescue also made famous the lifeboat involved, the 36500, a 36-foot motor lifeboat that transported 36 men through the storm and made Chatham the perfect place to test the next generation lifeboat, the 44-footer. Coast Guard Station Chatham remains operational today, in the building pictured. (United States Coast Guard.)

Although women were not allowed to go to sea with the Coast Guard until the 1970s, they did serve in other roles, especially during World War II. Here, the SPARS of Unit 21, Chatham, pose for their annual Christmas card photograph. The SPARS, a name formed from the Latin motto of the Coast Guard and its English translation (Semper Paratus, or Always Prepared), served as the Women's Reserve. SPARS trained in 30 different roles during the war, and at maximum strength reached 10,000 enlisted with 1,000 officers. That meant that of every 13 officers in the Coast Guard during World War II, one was a woman. Capt. Dorothy Stratton, the first commander of the SPARS, noted that a spar was a supporting beam on a ship, and that's what she wanted her SPARS to be for the Coast Guard. (Richard Ryder.)

Because of the ever-shifting sands of the Chatham Bar, the Coast Guard has gone to great lengths to be sure the crews serving at the local station have had the proper equipment. In 1962, Bernard "Bernie" Webber, the hero of the *Pendleton* rescue, transported the first 44-foot motor lifeboat up the coast from Maryland to Chatham. Thanks to its relatively flat keel, the boat worked well at Chatham. It was in use well into the 21st century, long after all of the others had been pulled out of service. Despite the obvious need for the best the service has to offer, the station has never had a 47-foot motor lifeboat; the propellers would never clear the bar. With such natural obstructions, it seems as if the Coast Guard will be in Chatham for decades to come. (Richard Ryder.)

The Pollock Rip lightship station marked the joining of the Pollock Rip and Pollock Rip Slue channels, seldom used today. The route was a shortcut, a way to avoid the Nantucket Shoals, but it came with regularly occurring heavy fog, especially in spring and summer. The Coast Guard last watched the shoals from a lightship in 1969. (Richard Ryder.)

The Stonehorse Shoal was originally named Shovelful Shoal by the locals and was the site of a terrible disaster in 1902. The barge *Wadena* stranded there, and the rescue crew from the Monomoy Point station responded, most losing their lives in the attempt. The last Stonehorse Shoal lightship, *WAL-524*, is now a museum ship in Portsmouth, Virginia. (United States Coast Guard.)

On August 29, 1970, the Coast Guard consolidated its southern New England air operations assets on the grounds of the Massachusetts Military Reservation. A reconfiguration of boundaries in 1977 established the station as a separate entity from Camp Edwards and the Otis Air National Guard Base. The original base assets consisted of HH-3F Pelicans and HU-16E Albatrosses transferred from Air Station Salem and its detachment at Quonset Point, Rhode Island, as well as HH-52A Sea Guard helicopters such as the one shown here. The Seaguards were eventually replaced in the early 1980s by HH-60 Jayhawks, still in use by the service today. This particular Sea Guard, number 1394, is now an exhibit at the Mid-Atlantic Air Museum in Reading, Pennsylvania. (United States Coast Guard.)

During the station's first 20 years, Coast Guardsmen from Air Station Cape Cod saved approximately 2,400 lives, including 37 from the sinking Russian ship *Komsomolets Kirgizzii* in March 1987. For their heroics, the crews of the three helicopters involved were thanked by Pres. Ronald Reagan in a White House Rose Garden ceremony. As the only Coast Guard air station in the northeast, the unit watches over all waters from New Jersey to the Canadian border, with a complement of four helicopters and four jets. Because of its large area of responsibility, Air Station Cape Cod performs search and rescue operations at a greater rate than the average station in the United States. And, because of its position near Stellwagen Bank and the great whale feeding grounds on the North Atlantic, the station spends a large amount of time ensuring the safety of marine animals. These duties and many others fall under the Coast Guard's five fundamental roles of maritime safety, maritime security, maritime mobility, national defense, and protection of natural resources. (United States Coast Guard.)

Whether by air or sea (or sometimes both), Coast Guardsmen on Cape Cod have lived up to their service's motto, *Semper Paratus*. Ready at a moment's notice to tackle any emergency, they have given their all, sometimes their lives, to save others. The same can be said of any Coast Guardsman at any unit in Massachusetts, from the North Shore to the South Coast to the islands. The sacrifices made by Coast Guardsmen in Massachusetts have been tremendous. Some rescues have made great headlines and endured the test of history. Others have been more or less lost to time. From small surfboats to motor lifeboats to modern day helicopters, the Coast Guard's assets have rescued thousands of people in distress off the shore of the Bay State. (United States Coast Guard.)

Six

THE RESCUES

The USS *Swan* (34), a Navy minesweeper, while trying to refloat a wrecked oil barge during a northeaster on Cape Cod Bay on November 28, 1920, was suddenly cast ashore at Plymouth's Gurnet Beach. The Coast Guard station at Gurnet rescued the crew of six with a breeches buoy and the surfboat. *Swan* was refloated on February 22, 1921. The *Swan* was at Pearl Harbor on December 7, 1941, and she fired on Japanese planes as they attacked. (Dick Boonisar.)

During a gale on March 9, 1928, the Eastern Steamship Line's Boston to New York steamship SS *Robert E. Lee*, with 273 passengers and crew, was grounded on Mary Ann Rocks southeast of Manomet Point, Plymouth. She was not damaged and in no danger of sinking. The crew of the Manomet Coast Guard Station did not know that there was no danger to the *Lee*. They reached the ship in their surfboat March 10. On the way, back a wave swamped the boat and three men died. (Old Colony Club.)

This is the crew of the Manomet Point Coast Guard Station preparing their surfboat to go out to the SS *Robert E. Lee*. Three of the men in this photograph will not come back alive. Boatswain's Mate William Cashman, Surfman Edward Stark, and Frank Griswold drowned when their boat was swamped. The *Robert E. Lee* was refloated. She was torpedoed and sunk by the German U-boat *U-166* in the Gulf of Mexico, July 30, 1942. (Old Colony Club.)

On June 10, 1930, off the coast of Scituate, the Merchants and Miners Transportation Company Passenger Steamship SS *Fairfax*, in thick fog, hit the gasoline tanker SS *Pinthis* of the Lake Tanker Corporation. On impact, the *Pinthis* caught fire and exploded and rained flames and debris over the *Fairfax* before she sank. This photograph is of the burning gasoline and debris left on the sea after the *Pinthis* sank. Because of the thick fog and the lack of an SOS request, the Scituate Coast Guard station did not respond until the next day. There was an inquiry and the Coast Guard was exonerated. (United States Coast Guard.)

On March 6, 1948, the New Bedford 84-foot scallop dragger *Cape Ann* was returning home after 11 days on Georges Bank. She had a five man crew and 700 gallons of scallops on board. She had mistaken Nauset Light for Pollock Rip Lightship and came ashore near Nauset Light in Eastham. The Coast Guard brought the crew ashore by breeches buoy. The captain stayed to salvage the scallops and some fishing gear. (United States Coast Guard.)

On February 18, 1952, two T-2 tankers broke in half in a northeaster (SS *Pendleton* and SS *Fort Mercer*). In this photograph is the stern section of the *Pendleton* as it looked after the rescue. The Chatham Coast Guard station sent out a 36-foot motor lifeboat under the command of Bernard Webber, boatswain's mate first class. They came upon the *Pendleton* and were able to rescue 32 out of the 33 who came down the Jacob's Ladder, jumped into the water, and were pulled into the boat. One crew member was lost in this operation. (United States Coast Guard.)

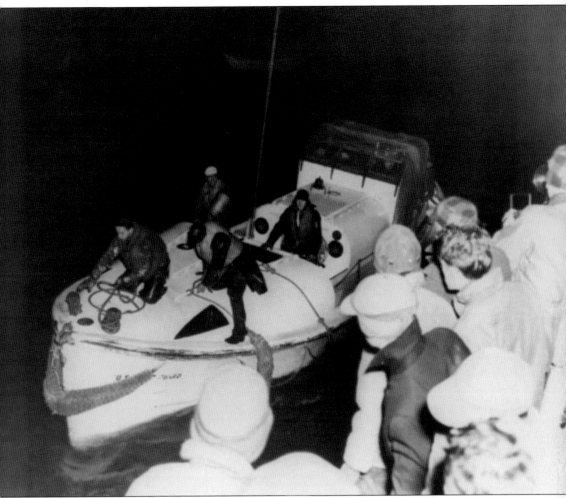

This is the return of the 36-foot motor lifeboat 36500 to the fish pier in Chatham. News of the rescues was out and people came to greet the boat. Besides the crew of four, there were 32 rescued seamen on board. On the way out, the lifeboat's windshield was broken and the compass was knocked off its mount by the rough seas. With one small searchlight and one small boat, this crew performed one big rescue. (United States Coast Guard.)

The SS *Fort Mercer* was farther offshore than the SS *Pendleton* and was able to give a radio distress signal. This brought cutters from Boston—the *Eastwind*, *Unimak*, *Boston*, and *Yakutat*—and a tug from Portland, Maine—the *Acushnet*—to the rescue. This photograph shows the cutter *Eastwind* passing the stern section of the *Fort Mercer*. (United States Coast Guard.)

The stern section of the *Fort Mercer* had drifted 20 miles away from the bow section. The *Eastwind* took some survivors off by running a rubber boat back and forth, but this proved risky because of the roll of the *Eastwind*, an icebreaker. The *Acushnet* was able to maneuver close enough to have men jump on to her deck, which was also risky. The *Unimak* launched a lifeboat, but it was nearly lost. (United States Coast Guard.)

The *Yakutat* is ferrying men to safety from the bow section of the *Fort Mercer* in a rubber boat. The last two crewmen were saved in this manner. Some 20 minutes later, the bow sank. A full 38 crewmembers were saved from the *Fort Mercer*. Of the 84 crewmembers on the two tankers, 70 were saved. Receiving decoration for saving lives of the crew of the two ships were 20 Coast Guardsmen. (United States Coast Guard.)

Hurricane Carol made landfall in southeastern Massachusetts on August 31, 1954. Its wind gusts were up to 125 miles per hour. In the New Bedford area, tidal surges were over 14 feet. Some of the damage the hurricane did to fishing boats in the harbor can be seen in this image. The small white boat in the photograph is likely the Coast Guard making an inspection of the damages. (United States Coast Guard.)

This Coast Guard 40-foot utility boat is inspecting the damage along New Bedford's waterfront caused by the wind and the hurricane's extreme tidal surge. In order to moderate such surges in the future, from 1958 to 1966 the Army Corps of Engineers built a hurricane barrier at the mouth of New Bedford Harbor. This barrier has a gate system that allows gates to be opened or shut when there is a danger of tidal surge. (United States Coast Guard)

This is Brant Island, located in Nasketucket Bay, part of Buzzards Bay, in the town of Mattapoisett. The causeway to the island was wiped out by Hurricane Carol. Residents were isolated and the Coast Guard came to their rescue. (United States Coast Guard.)

Genevieve Phipps, 83 years old of Valdosta, Illinois, was staying on Brant Island during Hurricane Carol and needed hospitalization. In this photograph, she is being evacuated by a Coast Guard crew and their DUKW, an amphibious vehicle known as the Duck. (United States Coast Guard.)

Hurricane Carol devastated coastal communities in southeastern Massachusetts. Some 4,000 cottages and 3,000 boats were lost. The Coast Guard, in addition to coming to the aid of storm victims, also performed shore duty to protect personal property from looters. (United States Coast Guard.)

This is the SS *Etrusco* as she looked when hard aground at Scituate after a snowstorm on March 16, 1956. She was built in 1942 as a Canadian version of a Liberty Ship. After World War II, she was sold to an Italian company and named SS *Etrusco*. At 8:10 p.m., the ship sent a radio call to the Coast Guard. At about 8:20 p.m., a Cedar Point resident called the Scituate Coast Guard Station to tell them that a large ship was coming ashore. (United States Coast Guard.)

The Scituate and the Point Allerton Coast Guard stations both responded to the radio call. On the morning of March 17, 1956, as the storm subsided, a breeches buoy line was attached to the ship and the Coast Guard started to take off the crew of 30. (United States Coast Guard.)

The *Etrusco*, along with Scituate Light, became a tourist destination, with thousands of visitors coming until she was refloated on Thanksgiving Day, November 22, 1956. The ship was renamed SS *Scituate* on December 7, 1956, in appreciation of the help and hospitality given by the people of Scituate. The ship was sold to Victor Transport, which sold in it 1961 to Blessing Sociedad. She was scrapped in 1964. (United States Coast Guard.)

The *Etrusco* landed in front of the cottage of Lena Russo. She opened her cottage to the Coast Guard as their field headquarters and to the rescued crew, with whom her fluent Italian was useful. Navy admiral Lebbeus Curtis used Russo's enclosed porch as his office during the refloating operation. The photograph shows Russo receiving a trophy from the Coast Guard and a flag from the *Etrusco*'s crew. (United States Coast Guard.)

The SS *Andrea Doria* was headed to New York on July 25, 1956, when she was hit about amidships on the portside by the MS *Stockholm*, which was heading out of New York, 50 miles south of Nantucket. The *Andrea Doria* took on water and listed to starboard, making it impossible to launch the portside lifeboats. The Coast Guard responded with cutters and helicopters. (United States Coast Guard.)

In this photograph, the *Andrea Doria* passengers have been evacuated and a Coast Guard cutter is standing by. Of those on the *Andrea Doria*, 46 lost their lives. Through the efforts of the Coast Guard, the SS *Ile de France*, other ships in the area, and the efforts of the passengers and crew, 1,660 were rescued. The *Stockholm* lost five. (United States Coast Guard.)

This is the Coast Guard buoy tender *Hornbeam*. She has two lifeboats from the *Andrea Doria*, which is low in the water in the background. *Hornbeam* will take the lifeboats to Woods Hole, her home port. Other Coast Guard cutters involved were *Tamaroa* of the Perfect Storm of October 1991, the *Owasco*, and the tug *Mahoning*. (United States Coast Guard.)

Here is the Coast Guard helicopter from Cape Cod evacuating the injured from the *Stockholm*. They took those in need of medical attention to Nantucket, where they were transferred to hospitals. Besides the five crew members killed as a result of the collision, two *Andrea Doria* passengers were killed as a result of the rescue operations. One badly injured person was found on the *Stockholm* who had been a passenger on the *Andrea Doria*. (United States Coast Guard.)

The *Stockholm* is being escorted by the Coast Guard tug *Mahoning* into New York Harbor. The *Tamaroa* also escorted *Stockholm* into New York. The *Andrea Doria* went down off Nantucket. The *Stockholm* was repaired and was sold in 1961 and named *Volkerfreundschaft*. She was sold again, and as of the publishing date of this book, she sails as the MV *Athena*. (United States Coast Guard.)

This is a four-alarm fire at the White Fuel Oil Company piers near Castle Island, Boston, on December 1, 1961. The boat is the Coast Guard *40417*, ordered by the captain of the port to assist. There were 200 firemen and policemen fighting this fire. (United States Coast Guard.)

On December 31, 1962, during a storm of subzero temperatures, snow, high winds, and a lack of visibility, the 87-foot dragger *Katie D* lost power and drifted. She grounded on Rocky Neck, Gloucester. The Coast Guard was called and rescued eight fishermen. (United States Coast Guard.)

Pictured is the Gloucester Coast Guard Station's 36-foot motor lifeboat that went out to rescue the fishermen on the *Katie D*. Because of the terrible conditions, she went aground on Niles Beach, Gloucester. Her crew was able to get off the boat safely. (United States Coast Guard.)

On December 16, 1962, the fishing vessel *Margaret Rose* became disabled and ran aground at Wood End Light, at Race Point in Provincetown. The Race Point Coast Guard Station crew responded. A breeches buoy was set up and seven crew members were saved from the fishing vessel. (United States Coast Guard.)

The Coast Guard, from 1948 to the 1970s, used a version of the Army's DUKW (or Duck). The prototypes were tested near Provincetown by the Army in 1942. The Coast Guard version was 38 feet long and had an aluminum body. One can see the Ducks from the Race Point station in both photographs on this page, which were taken by a Coast Guard helicopter. (United States Coast Guard.)

On November 14, 1963, at 7:00 a.m. and in patchy fog, the Norwegian freighter *Fernview* ran into the portside of the Sun Oil tanker *Dynafuel*. This took place on Buzzards Bay between Cuttyhunk Island and South Dartmouth. Both ships caught fire. The *Fernview* had a crew of 40 and sustained no injuries. The *Dynafuel* had a crew of 22, and 5 were slightly injured. The crew of the tanker was able to escape to the freighter. (United States Coast Guard.)

This view of the *Fernview-Dynafuel* collision shows the *General Greene*, two Coast Guard cutters, and a boat all fighting the fire. The cutter *Legare*, which was a patrol boat from New Bedford, and the *White Sage*, which was a coastal buoy tender from Woods Hole, responded to fight the fire, as did several small boats. Coast Guard helicopters from Salem were working all day providing foam to fight the fire. (United States Coast Guard.)

The men of the *General Greene* are aboard *Dynafuel* fighting the fire. Men from the *White Sage* were on the *Fernview* fighting the fire. *White Sage* and *Legare* put water on the portside of the tanker to cool it down. In the late afternoon, the fire was controlled. The cutters *Humbolt* and *Hornbeam* arrived to tow the ships to safety. Commercial tugs arrived and took over the salvage of the ships. The Coast Guard returned to their stations, a job well done. (United States Coast Guard.)

On December 15, 1976, the Liberian-flagged tanker *Argo Merchant* went aground in bad weather on Middle Rip Shoals, about 29 miles southeast of Nantucket. The crew of 38 was taken off the tanker. Neither the ship nor its cargo of almost eight million gallons of number six fuel could be salvaged. The cutter *Vigilant*, in this image, served as on-scene commander for the *Argo Merchant* salvaging. The cutter *Sherman* from Boston was also on duty at this wreck. (United States Coast Guard.)

The helicopter *1438*, an HH-3 Pelican, arrived from the Cape Cod Air Station. It brought the salvage team seen on the forward section of the *Argo Merchant* and took the men off the ship. (United States Coast Guard.)

In this photograph, the helicopter is still over the ship. The seas are not calm, and as time goes on, they will rise. This is the calm before the storm of a potential environmental disaster and action to combat such an occurrence. (United States Coast Guard.)

On December 21, 1976, the *Argo Merchant* broke in half, spilling its entire contents of oil into the sea—"enough oil to heat 18,000 homes for a year." The oil washed out to sea and did little harm to the coast. The spill, the biggest to date, motivated the government to pass stronger laws on tanker safety and environmental protection. At this point, the cutters *Spar* from Portsmouth, New Hampshire, and *Bittersweet* from Woods Hole were sent to help with the situation. (United States Coast Guard.)

These men were honored for their bravery in the *Argo Merchant* disaster on May 4, 1977. In this photograph are, from left to right, David Radina, Chief Joe Bayko, Claude Poirier, Russell Kassin, and Leo Clark. They are from the Merrimack River Station, Newburyport. Their faces are the faces of Coast Guard heroism—youthful and confident. (United States Coast Guard.)

For nearly 100 years, the United States Coast Guard has performed extreme acts of valor along the Massachusetts coast, using line-throwing cannons, helicopters, lifeboats, seaplanes, and sometimes nothing but their bare hands to save lives. As long as the political entity known as the Commonwealth of Massachusetts exists, it will share a love-hate relationship with the sea. During the good times, Massachusetts residents rush to the ocean to play, from its edge to its depths. When times are bad, they retreat. But it is at those times, when everyone else is running from it, that the Coast Guard takes to it, risking their lives and well being to save people they have never met. Can we imagine life on the Massachusetts coast without the Coast Guard? Here's to the hope that Bay Staters will never have to. (United States Coast Guard.)

www.arcadiapublishing.com

Discover books about the town where you grew up, the cities where your friends and families live, the town where your parents met, or even that retirement spot you've been dreaming about. Our Web site provides history lovers with exclusive deals, advanced notification about new titles, e-mail alerts of author events, and much more.

Arcadia Publishing, the leading local history publisher in the United States, is committed to making history accessible and meaningful through publishing books that celebrate and preserve the heritage of America's people and places. Consistent with our mission to preserve history on a local level, this book was printed in South Carolina on American-made paper and manufactured entirely in the United States.

This book carries the accredited Forest Stewardship Council (FSC) label and is printed on 100 percent FSC-certified paper. Products carrying the FSC label are independently certified to assure consumers that they come from forests that are managed to meet the social, economic, and ecological needs of present and future generations.

FSC
Mixed Sources
Product group from well-managed
forests and other controlled sources

Cert no. SW-COC-001530
www.fsc.org
© 1996 Forest Stewardship Council

Find Your Place in History.